Sign Language & Food

Bela Davis

Abdo Kids Junior
is an Imprint of Abdo Kids
abdobooks.com

Abdo
EVERYDAY SIGN LANGUAGE
Kids

abdobooks.com

Published by Abdo Kids, a division of ABDO, P.O. Box 398166, Minneapolis, Minnesota 55439.

Printed in the United States of America, North Mankato, Minnesota.

052021

092021

THIS BOOK CONTAINS RECYCLED MATERIALS

Photo Credits: iStock, Shutterstock

Production Contributors: Teddy Borth, Jennie Forsberg, Grace Hansen

Design Contributors: Candice Keimig, Pakou Moua

Library of Congress Control Number: 2020947530

Publisher's Cataloging-in-Publication Data

Names: Davis, Bela, author.

Title: Sign language & food / by Bela Davis

Description: Minneapolis, Minnesota : Abdo Kids, 2022 | Series: Everyday sign language | Includes online resources and index.

Identifiers: ISBN 9781098207021 (lib. bdg.) | ISBN 9781098207861 (ebook) | ISBN 9781098208288 (Read-to-Me ebook)

Subjects: LCSH: American Sign Language--Juvenile literature. | Food--Juvenile literature. | Eating--Juvenile literature. | Deaf--Means of communication--Juvenile literature. | Language acquisition--Juvenile literature.

Classification: DDC 419--dc23

Table of Contents

Signs and Food

ASL is a visual language. When it is time to eat, there is a sign for every food!

EAT/FOOD

1. Press four closed, flat fingers to thumb
2. Tap fingers to mouth

Abe is very hungry today.

He eats a lot!

HUNGRY

1. Make “C” sign with one hand
2. Touch fingertips to chest and pull down toward tummy

Pam picks peas. The peas taste sweet.

PEAS

1. Hold one hand at chest height with pointer finger extended and other fingers tucked in
2. Curve other hand's pointer finger and tuck other fingers in
3. Tap the curved finger several times on the straight finger from bottom to tip

Arie likes cheese on her pizza.

CHEESE

1. Bring both hands up with fingers slightly apart
2. Press the palms together
3. Twist wrists back and forth in opposite directions

Sam's favorite treat is
cookies and cold milk.

MILK

1. Bring one hand up in a fist
2. Open and close the fist a few times, like milking a cow

The corn is **ripe**.

James helps pick it.

CORN

1. Hold hands up near mouth as if holding an ear of corn
2. Slide hands from side to side while making a biting motion

Lea and Betty bake bread.

They use lots of flour.

BREAD

1. Bring one hand up, fingers together and palm facing body to look like a bread loaf
2. Bring the other, curved hand, up and act as if slicing the other hand with the tips of the fingers

Danny learns to make a sushi roll. The rice helps it stay together.

RICE

1. Put hand in front of body with palm curved and facing up like it is a bowl
2. Make the “R” sign with the other hand and touch it to palm and up to mouth

Sara is full. Her mom made a big dinner!

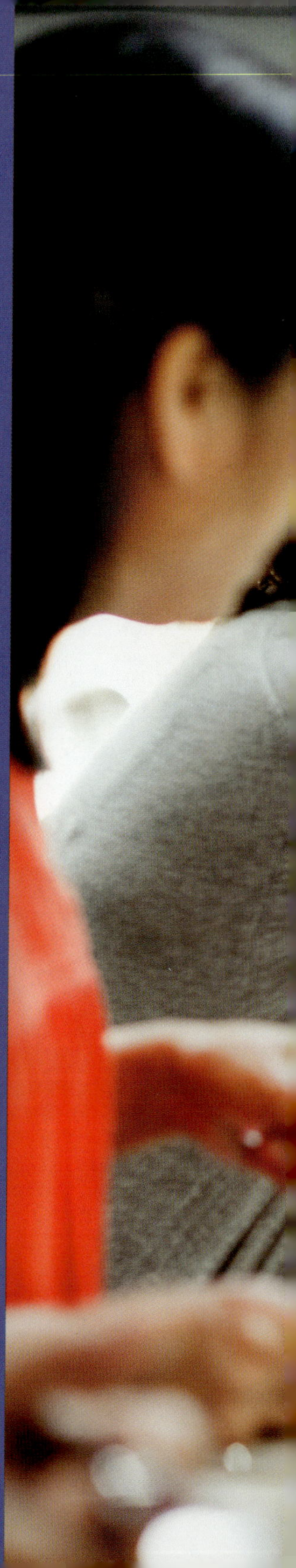

FULL

1. Start with one flat hand at waist height, palm facing down
2. Bring the hand up to just under the chin

The ASL Alphabet!

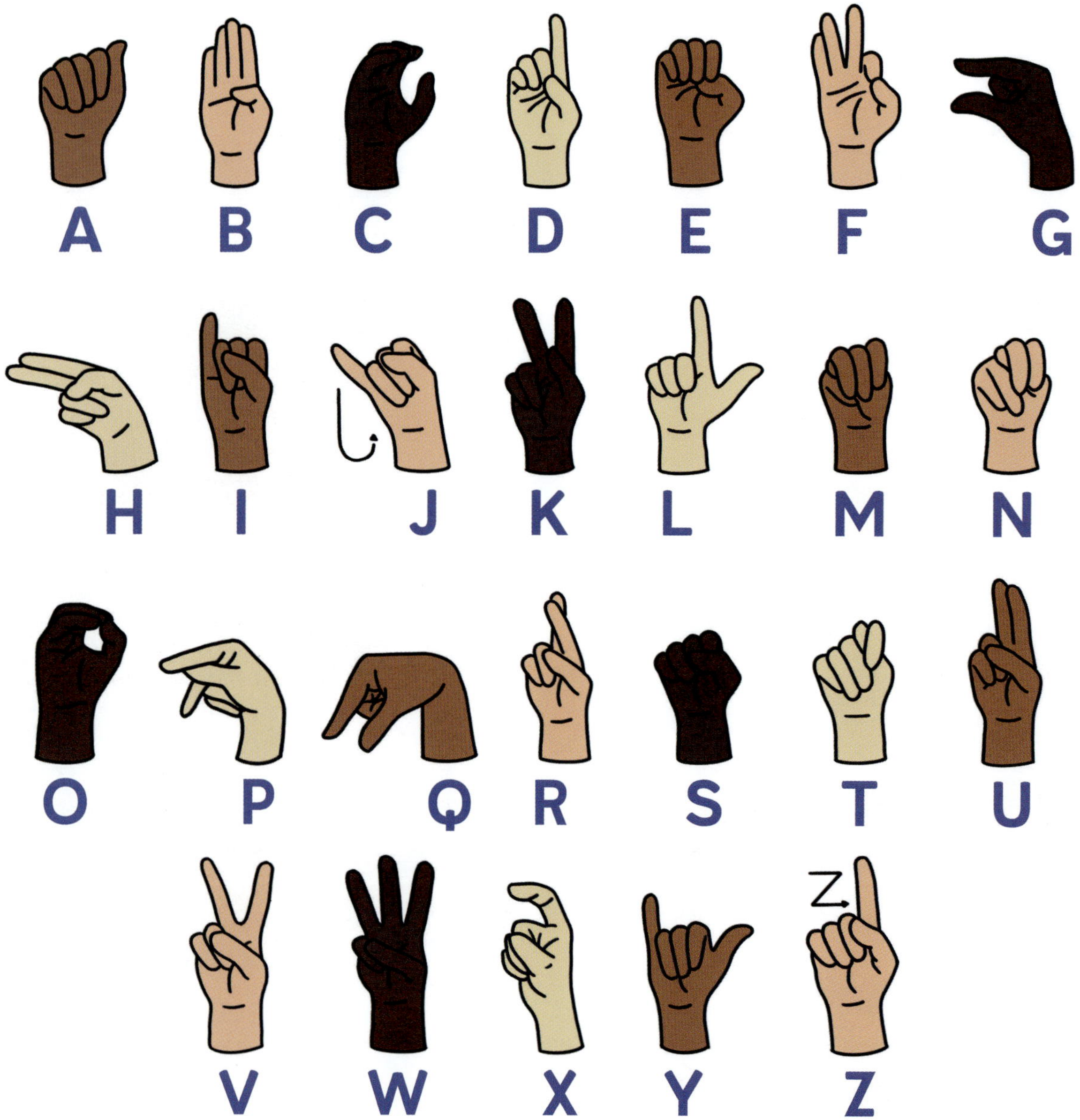

Glossary

ASL
short for American Sign Language, a language used by many deaf people in North America.

ripe
fully grown and ready for eating.

Index